GLOW-IN-THE-DARK
Creatures

GLOW-IN-THE-DARK
Creatures

by NATALIE HYDE

Fitzhenry & Whiteside

To Craig, who thought nothing of dropping everything
and driving me nine hours each way to see the
Creatures of Light exhibit for research.

A grateful acknowledgement goes to Dr. Leo Smith and Dr. Matt Davis
at the Field Museum, Chicago, for taking time from their busy schedules
to meet with me and answer all my questions. Also to Dr. Dimitri Deheyn
at the Scripps Institution of Oceanography for sharing his expertise
and photographs of *Hinea brasiliana*. Thanks also go to Solange Messier,
Christie Harkin, Cheryl Chen, Winston Stilwell, and everyone else at
Fitzhenry & Whiteside for their enthusiasm and care in putting this book together.
Finally, I would also like to thank Craig for his help with the facts and figures,
Haley for giving me a reader's perspective, and Chelsey
for her patience and photographic skill with the activities in this book.

Copyright © 2014 Natalie Hyde

Published in Canada by Fitzhenry & Whiteside,
195 Allstate Parkway, Markham, ON L3R 4T8

Published in the United States by Fitzhenry & Whiteside,
311 Washington Street, Brighton, Massachusetts 02135

10 9 8 7 6 5 4 3 2 1

Fitzhenry & Whiteside acknowledges with thanks the Canada Council for the Arts,
and the Ontario Arts Council for their support of our publishing program.
We acknowledge the financial support of the Government of Canada through
the Canada Book Fund (CBF) for our publishing activities.

Library and Archives Canada Cataloguing in Publication
Glow in the Dark Creatures
ISBN 978-1-55455-330-3 (Hardcover)
Data available on file

Publisher Cataloging-in-Publication Data (U.S.)
Glow in the Dark Creatures
ISBN 978-1-55455-330-3 (Hardcover)
Data available on file

Text and cover design by Tanya Montini
Front cover image courtesy of Terry Priest/Visuals Unlimited, Inc.
Printed in China by Sheck Wah Tong Printing Press Ltd.

CONTENTS

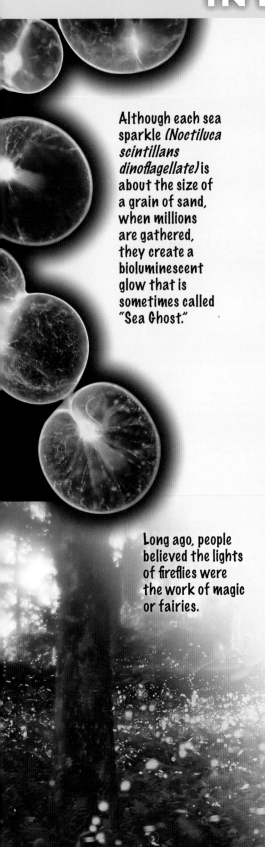

Although each sea sparkle (*Noctiluca scintillans dinoflagellate*) is about the size of a grain of sand, when millions are gathered, they create a bioluminescent glow that is sometimes called "Sea Ghost."

Long ago, people believed the lights of fireflies were the work of magic or fairies.

The Remarkable World of Bioluminescence

From the skies above us to the deepest oceans, our world is full of twinkling, flashing, blinking, and glowing lights. Whether it is the gentle dance of fireflies in the air or the explosion of colours and patterns in the deep sea, this light show is the silent language of remarkable creatures.

"Bio" means life or living; "luminescence" means light. Creatures that can produce this living light are said to be bioluminescent. This ability is such a useful tool for survival that it is used by many different kinds of creatures, both on land and in the sea. Scientists believe the proof of how effective bioluminescence is lies in the fact that it did not **evolve** just once or twice—it evolved separately more than 40 times.

DOWN IN THE DEEP

While several kinds of land creatures can create their own light, most bioluminescent creatures live in the sea. In fact, now that scientists know how and where to look in the deep sea, they are finding new bioluminescent creatures all the time. They are also learning that the twinkling and flashing is not a random show, but a way to communicate. If scientists can crack the code to their meaning, imagine the conversations we could have!

BIOLUMINESCENCE ON LAND

Only 20% of bioluminescent creatures live on land; the rest live in the oceans. The evolution of bioluminescence takes a long time, and land animals haven't been around as long as marine animals. The chemicals that create light are also **toxic**. Creatures in the sea can easily get rid of these toxins by swimming away, but land animals have to develop a way to get rid of the residue that could harm their bodies.

FOXFIRE

In ancient times, people noticed mysterious lights coming from logs and trees in the forest. Greek philosopher Aristotle was the first to mention this "cold light" in his writings. Ancient Scandinavians would gather the glowing bark and mushrooms and use them as cold-light lanterns in places where a flame might start a fire. Often, the light was so bright that they could use it inside their homes during the long, dark winters.

Sometimes, wooden beams supporting walls and ceilings deep in mines glowed. People believed that these lights were made by dragons, gods, or ghosts. They called the gentle glowing "foxfire" or sometimes "fairy fire." Japanese folktales tell stories of trickster foxes that used glowing lights to lead foolish travellers or greedy merchants from the road, so they would become lost in the woods. For the Welsh, fairies were the mischievous ones that created the lights, which they called "will-o'-the-wisp."

SEA FIRE

Since ancient times, seafarers have also seen strange lights in the water. They told stories of sparkling seas and sea fire. They noticed bright blue flashes exploding as they dipped their oars in seawater. Even Christopher Columbus mentioned strange lights floating on the water as he neared the coast of San Salvador.

Ancient people recognized how much safer and more efficient "cold light" from bioluminescence was over regular lanterns.

This Red Tide in La Jolla Cove, California, was formed by an algal bloom. Thousands of tiny dinoflagellates turned the water red by day, and glowed blue at night.

CHIMPANZEE FIRE

Scientists have recently discovered a new species of bioluminescent fungus in the Congo region of Africa. Local people called the fungus "Chimpanzee Fire," perhaps from an ancient belief that the chimpanzees were responsible for the glowing lights in the jungle.

BIRDS OF A FEATHER

Long ago, Roman naturalist Pliny the Elder wrote that there were bioluminescent birds in the Black Forest in Germany. This idea persisted for over a thousand years, but no glowing birds have ever been found. Others claim that some barn owls are bioluminescent, but so far scientists cannot prove the existence of any bioluminescent birds.

LET THERE BE LIGHT

Bioluminescence seems like an amazing trick. Using nothing but their bodies, animals can produce a light show that is not only useful, but also beautiful. So, how do these creatures create their own light?

Bioluminescence is a chemical reaction. It needs three different ingredients to work: luciferin, luciferase, and oxygen. Luciferin and luciferase both contain the Latin word *lucifer*, which means "bringer of light."

THE INGREDIENTS FOR BIOLUMINESCENCE

Luciferin is not one single chemical; it is the term for any chemical compound that can be used to produce light. Different creatures have different types of luciferin. Some make luciferin in their bodies, others have to take it in from their environment.

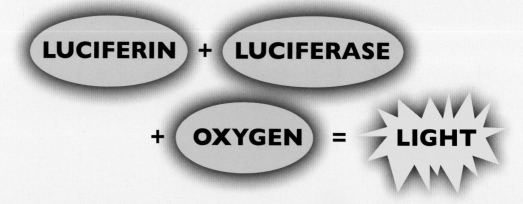

LUCIFERIN + LUCIFERASE + OXYGEN = LIGHT

Luciferase is an enzyme, which is a **molecule** that helps reactions happen. Enzymes are like assembly-line robots in a car factory. They help the work get done quickly and efficiently. Each robot has a different task: some lift engines, some attach doors, and some screw in bolts. Every enzyme in the body also has a specific job. The job of luciferase is to combine luciferin with oxygen.

Oxygen is a gas that is found both in our atmosphere and in water. In bioluminescence, oxygen is like the spark that ignites the chemical reaction. Some creatures need to add another element to their oxygen in order to work. This is called the co-factor. Fireflies need ATP (Adenosine triphosphate), some jellyfish need calcium ions, and bioluminescent earthworms need hydrogen peroxide.

While ATP is found in all the firefly's cells, luciferin and luciferase are located in only one spot on its body. The end of its abdomen where these chemicals are found is called a "lantern."

GETTING IT ALL TOGETHER

When all these elements are combined, the energy from the chemical reaction is released as light and oxyluciferin is left over. The light that bioluminescent creatures produce is measured in units called photons. Tiny bioluminescent creatures called dinoflagellates can give off 1,010 photons per second. When millions of these organisms are packed together on the surface of the ocean, the light can be very bright!

Some bioluminescent organisms, like bacteria, make all the ingredients for the reaction themselves. Other creatures make everything except luciferin, which they take from the surrounding water or from their food. Still others, such as the flashlight fish, have organs in their bodies that contain bioluminescent bacteria, which do the work for them.

COLD LIGHT

Bioluminescence is called cold light because the energy released from the chemical reaction is almost totally light, and not heat. Light bulbs waste a lot of energy by giving off heat as well as light. Ordinary light bulbs give off up to 90% of their energy as heat and only 10% as light. Bioluminescence is the most efficient reaction, producing almost 100% light.

It would take hundreds of millions of dinoflagellates all flashing at the once to equal the output of a 100-watt light bulb.

CHAPTER I

Fireflies live in moist, warm environments. They can be found on every continent except Antarctica.

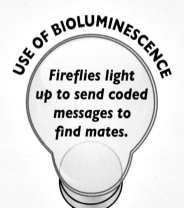

USE OF BIOLUMINESCENCE

Fireflies light up to send coded messages to find mates.

Sparkling Skies

On warm summer evenings in many parts of the world, the skies above us come to life with the dance of the fireflies. Tiny flickering lights are more than just a pretty display; they are conversations between the flying insects.

FLIGHT OF LIGHT

Fireflies are not flies. They are winged members of the beetle family *Lampyridae*. They spend their short, two-month lives in warm, wet environments around the world. They earned their name by using special cells at the end of their bodies to produce light. Turning this light on and off in a pattern of flashes is a little like **Morse code**, but uses light instead of sound. Each species of firefly has its own special code, and this helps fireflies recognize each other when it comes time to find a mate.

PUTTING ON A SHOW

Usually, only the males fly around while the females watch from branches or rocks. Male fireflies often hover in one place so their bioluminescent tails can be seen more clearly by the females. When a female sees a pattern that she likes, she sends out her own answering flash. The male zooms to her side and they mate. A little later, she will lay eggs and a new generation of dancing lights will develop.

FEMALE FAKERS

Sometimes, a female *Photuris* firefly will copy the flash patterns of another species. Males see her **beckoning** and think they've found a mate. When the lovestruck males land beside her, she eats them.

BLUE GHOSTS

One type of firefly is known as the "blue ghost." Instead of creating a flickering yellow light, this species emits a bluish glow. As it floats at knee height in the darkness, its bioluminescent behind makes little streaks of light. Blue ghosts are only found in a few places on the planet, mainly in the southern Appalachian Mountains of the United States.

How to Catch a Firefly

1. Turn off any outdoor lights; they might confuse the fireflies.

2. Use an LED flashlight to attract the fireflies by imitating their flash patterns. Never shine a light directly at them or you might scare them away.

3. Have a clear jar ready with holes punched in the lid for air. Put a damp paper towel in the bottom of the jar to keep the air inside the jar moist.

4. Catch fireflies carefully in a net—they are delicate and crush easily.

5. Gently transfer them from the net to the jar.

6. Keep them only for a day or so, otherwise they will die. Let them go at night near where you found them.

EVOLUTION OF BIOLUMINESCENT FIREFLIES

Scientists believe that the earliest fireflies didn't glow at all. Then, fireflies developed the ability to produce light and glowed constantly. Next, their light began to pulse slowly on and off. Finally, fireflies gained the ability to control the length and speed of their flashes.

TWINKLE, TWINKLE, LITTLE DEATH TRAP

In the quiet darkness of a cave, an unbelievable light show takes place. Below is a deep, dark river and overhead is what looks like thousands of little blue stars. This beautiful sparkling ceiling is the work of New Zealand glowworms.

LOVE MATCH

Male and female fireflies in each species have their own unique flash patterns. The males have to know which pattern belongs to a female of their own species. Can you guess which female pattern will answer this male carolinus firefly's signal?

Male carolinus firefly: X X X X X X
Female A: X X X X X
Female B: XX XX XX
Female C: XXXXXX

Female B is correct. The female carolinus firefly uses two quick flashes together, followed by a pause.

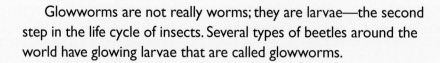

Glowworms are not really worms; they are larvae—the second step in the life cycle of insects. Several types of beetles around the world have glowing larvae that are called glowworms.

SPIDER WORMS

One type of glowworm, called the *Arachnocampa,* which means "spider worm," is only found in parts of Australia and New Zealand. This larva will grow into a small flying insect called a gnat. While it is in larva form, the *Arachnocampa* lives in shady and humid caves, under rock ledges or creek banks, or in cracks in cliffs. Only 3 centimetres (1 inch) long, it can make a bright blue-green glow in its tail.

It eats mosquitos, fruit flies, and midges, and it uses an **ingenious** trap to catch its prey. First, the glowworm spins a silky tube on the ceiling to hide in. All around, it hangs long threads dotted with sticky mucus that acts like glue. In outside areas, the silky threads are not too long so they don't get tangled, but on the ceilings of caves where there is no wind, they can be up to 100 centimetres (40 inches) long. After it hangs as many as seventy of these sticky silk threads, the glowworm crawls back in its tube and turns on its light. The bright light attracts flying insects, which then get caught in the sticky droplets. When it feels movement on its web, the glowworm finds the jiggling thread and pulls up its meal with its mouth.

CAVES OF WONDER

The Waitomo Caves in New Zealand are home to thousands of the *Arachnocampa* glowworms. The caves were discovered over one hundred years ago by Maori chief Tane Tinorau and an English **surveyor,** Fred Mace. They built a raft of flax stems and used candlelight to follow the river as it went down into the caves. They were astounded at the beauty of the tiny lights on the cave ceiling. Today, tours allow visitors to walk and take boat rides through the cave system and marvel at the glittering display overhead.

DISMALITES

These glowworms are close cousins to the New Zealand glowworms and make their home in a secluded canyon in Alabama, United States. Dismalites are the bioluminescent larva of the *Orfelia fultoni* beetle. They hang their sticky webs from the moss-covered walls of Dismals Canyon.

Glowworms use their bioluminescent lights to mimic the stars. This creates the illusion of an open sky and lures insects.

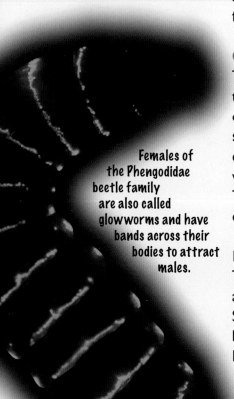

Females of the Phengodidae beetle family are also called glowworms and have bands across their bodies to attract males.

THE RAILROAD WORM

The railroad worm is another type of glowing larva. It will grow up to be an adult *Phrixothrix* beetle. It earned its nickname by having two different bioluminescent colours—it has two red lights on its head like headlights, and pairs of yellow lights down its body that look like the lit windows of train cars. Scientists discovered that the different colours are formed by two different kinds of luciferase in the larvae's body.

HANDLE WITH CARE!

Visitors need to be careful when touring the caves:

* ✳ Glowworms are affected by light. Too much light from flashlights can make them hide in a crack or hole and starve to death.

* ✳ The flash from cameras can kill glowworms. The bright light can injure their delicate eyes.

* ✳ Glowworms are insects and can be harmed by insect repellents and even strong perfumes.

* ✳ Tobacco smoke contains nicotine, which is poisonous to insects.

* ✳ Warmer cave temperatures from the body heat of large groups of visitors can dry out and kill glowworms.

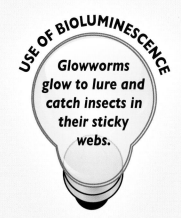

USE OF BIOLUMINESCENCE

Glowworms glow to lure and catch insects in their sticky webs.

A Scientific Advisory Group monitors conditions such as air quality, temperature, and carbon dioxide levels in the Waitomo Caves to protect the thousands of glowworms that live there.

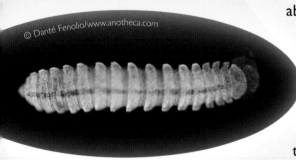

CHAPTER 2

The millipede's bioluminescent warning can easily be seen by nocturnal predators.

© Danté Fenolio/www.anotheca.com

Glittering Ground

Even below our feet, the world is alive with glowing creatures. Creeping, crawling, and burrowing in dark corners of the ground, they use their bioluminescence to hide, scare, or **distract**. It's all about surviving.

THE GLOW MEANS NO

In some parts of California, United States, a little millipede is sending out a warning: *I am poisonous—eat at your own risk*. It has a couple of special weapons it uses to stay alive: poison and light. Like other members of the *Motyxia* millipede family, this orange-pink, 3-centimetre (1-inch) long insect oozes cyanide from pores running along the sides of its body. Cyanide is an odorless, poisonous liquid that, in high doses, can kill a human in about one minute.

These millipedes are one of the few land creatures that are bioluminescent. Exactly why they produce light originally puzzled scientists because these millipedes are blind. If they can't see the light themselves, it can't be used for signaling mates or as camouflage. One scientist, Dr. Paul Marek, thought that they must use their bioluminescence to advertise that they are not good to eat. He devised an experiment to prove that their light shows were another way of scaring away nighttime **predators**.

MILLIPEDE IN THE MOONLIGHT

Dr. Paul Marek wanted to understand why blind millipedes would use light to communicate. He believed it must be used as a warning to keep predators away and set out to prove it. Dr. Marek began his experiment by making 300 fake millipedes out of clay. He painted half of those with long-lasting glow-in-the-dark paint and left the other half plain. He placed the painted and non-painted clay millipedes in random order on the ground in Giant Sequoia National Monument in California. Then, he collected real millipedes. He painted half of them to cover their bioluminescence and left the other half natural.

The next day he went out to collect both the live and clay millipedes. He and his team were shocked to see that so many of the millipedes had been eaten. More interesting was the fact that the non-glowing millipedes were eaten up to four times more

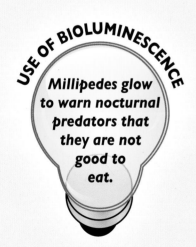

USE OF BIOLUMINESCENCE

Millipedes glow to warn nocturnal predators that they are not good to eat.

READING LIGHT

Click beetles get their name from their ability to make a loud clicking noise as they bend their spine and snap it back. By doing this, the beetles are able to bounce into the air to escape predators. They also have two spots on their backs near their heads that glow a bright green. On some islands in the Caribbean where the beetles live, islanders used to tie a few beetles to their toes to light their way at night. Prussian explorer Friedrich Humboldt noticed that he could read quite easily by the light of a dozen beetles.

Scientists have discovered that click beetles can make four different colours of bioluminescent light: green, yellow-green, yellow, and orange.

often than the bioluminescent ones. This helped prove their theory that the glowing was an effective way for millipedes to warn off predators and protect themselves.

ATTENTION SEEKER

If you take a walk in the woods at night, you might see a gentle glow on the dark forest floor. This eerie light is given off by bioluminescent mushrooms, such as the bitter oyster mushroom.

Mushrooms are fungi. They are neither plants nor animals, but something in between. They have stems and fruit bodies like plants, but must get their nutrition from other organisms, like animals. Some species of fungi are bioluminescent. They do not give off bright flashes of light like some animals, but glow steadily. Their glow might be faint, but it lasts for days.

Scientists are still unravelling the chemical process that occurs within bioluminescent fungi. Because the same chemicals that make bioluminescence work are also toxic, scientists believe this glow is a warning for **foragers** to stay away.

Scientists have found that the glow of bitter oyster mushrooms fades when it is exposed to toxins. They hope to use this ability to help detect soil pollution.

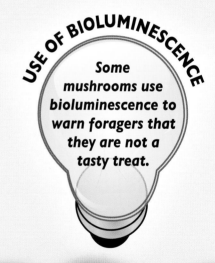

USE OF BIOLUMINESCENCE

Some mushrooms use bioluminescence to warn foragers that they are not a tasty treat.

USE OF BIOLUMINESCENCE

It is not only a warning, but also a way of putting a spotlight on a predator.

"It could be the snail's way of saying, 'hey—eat that guy—he's attacking me.'"

Dr. Dimitri Deheyn, marine biologist

CURIOUS CLUSTER

Living both in and out of the water at the edge of the sea is a bioluminescent creature that has puzzled scientists for years. A small snail has developed a special shell that acts not only as its home, but also like a frosted light bulb.

The tiny snail is found in clustered groups along the rocky shores of eastern Australia. The size of a thumbnail, it has found a unique way to use its shell and its bioluminescence to protect itself.

SPECIAL SHELL

While other snails may leave a glowing slime trail, the clusterwink snail, or *Hinea brasiliana*, flashes its blue-green light from one spot on its squishy body. Normally, a snail's shell would cover this light, but the clusterwink snail has a shell that lets light shine through. Scientists also found that while the shell glowed blue-green light, when they tried red or yellow lights inside the shell, it remained dark. The shell had developed to only allow the snail's blue-green bioluminescence to shine through. What's more, the design of the shell actually strengthened the light and spread it all around so that the whole shell glowed, like a light bulb.

Scientists believe clusterwink snails use their light as a way of bringing attention to an attacker, like security lights shining outside of a home to catch a burglar in the act. This way, larger predators can see and eat the attackers before the snails become a meal.

The flash of the clusterwink snail is extremely fast—pulsing ten times per second.

Make Your Own Glow-in-the-Dark Slime

Supplies Needed:
- ✦ 120 ml (4 oz) white glue
- ✦ water
- ✦ Borax powder
- ✦ teaspoon
- ✦ bowl
- ✦ plastic containers and measuring cup
- ✦ glow-in-the-dark paint

1. Pour the glue into a plastic container.

2. Add ½ cup of water.

3. Add 4 teaspoons (20 ml) of glow-in-the-dark paint.

4. In a separate container, mix 1 cup (240 ml) of water and add 1 teaspoon (5 ml) of Borax powder.

5. Slowly stir the glue mixture into the container of Borax solution.

6. Place the slime into your hands and knead it until it feels dry. (Don't worry about any extra water in the bowl.)

7. The more the slime is played with, the firmer and less sticky it will become.

8. Let your slime absorb sunlight for approximately 30 minutes. Watch your slime glow in a dark room or under black light.

9. Store your slime in a resealable bag in the refrigerator (otherwise it will go mouldy).

CHAPTER 3

The Sea's Sunlight Zone

The sea is divided into different layers depending on how much light can filter into the water. In the top layer, known as the Sunlight Zone (also called the Euphotic Zone), organisms can still use sunlight to see their prey or make their own food through photosynthesis. Photosynthesis is the process where plants take light, water, and carbon dioxide and make sugar (as their food) and oxygen. This zone goes down about 200 metres (650 feet) into the sea. Farther down, in the Twilight Zone, (or Disphotic Zone) only a small amount of light can get through. The depth of the Twilight Zone is from 200 metres (650 feet) to about 1,000 metres (3,300 feet). Below the Twilight Zone is the Midnight Zone (or Aphotic Zone). Here, no light can **penetrate**, and creatures that live here have never seen sunlight.

SEA SPECTACLES

If you are sailing out on a moonless night in the Indian Ocean, particularly in August or January, you might see an eerie blue glow surrounding your boat in the water. Sailors called this "sailing on milky seas," a **spectacle** created by billions of creatures too small for the naked eye to see.

MILKY SEAS

Scientists believe the milky seas are the work of bioluminescent bacteria, like *Vibrio harveyi*. Bacteria tend to glow and not flash, but their glow is faint. It takes huge numbers of bacteria coming together to produce the light described by sailors. When scientists found satellite images of the milky seas reported by the SS *Lima* in 1995, they were astounded. The patch of bioluminescent water was 15,400 square kilometres (6,000 square miles) in size: almost as large as Lake Ontario.

The dinoflagellates *Noctiluca scintillans* twinkles when it is disturbed, earning it the nickname "sea sparkle."

How many bacteria would it take to make this large an area of milky-coloured seas? Approximately four billion trillion, or the number 4 followed by 21 zeroes.

SPARKLING WAVES

Another bioluminescent microbe in the sea is the dinoflagellate, which means "whirling whips." Dinoflagellates are tiny one-celled creatures with long tails that they whip from side to side to move around. Many dinoflagellates can make their own light. Sailors would notice this light show as they rowed. Each time their oar hit the water, the surface would burst into bright blue sparks.

Many bioluminescent dinoflagellates live near Vieques Island, which is off the coast of Puerto Rico. Because there is only a narrow exit to the sea from the bay, most of the *Pyrodinium bahamense* dinoflagellates are forced to stay within its shallow waters. Visitors can kayak or use quiet electric boats to view the light show. At one time, the light from the bay was bright enough to allow people to read books on shore.

QUORUM SENSING

Scientists noticed that some tiny microorganisms seemed to be able to communicate with each other in order to move and act as one. These creatures only produced light where there were millions or billions of them gathered together. Scientists believe they use **quorum** sensing to communicate. In quorum sensing, an organism sends out a small signal. If it gets only a few responses, it waits. Once it gets many signals back, it knows to act. Dinoflagellates may use this system in order to begin glowing at the same time.

USE OF BIOLUMINESCENCE

Dinoflagellates use it as a burglar alarm to startle predators.

Because of the way our eyes see in the dark, milky seas look white, but they are actually blue.

COMB JELLIES

The sunlight that pierces the surface of the ocean creates an environment that allows many marine creatures to thrive. The comb jellies, or ctenophores, make up one family of creatures that lives in the Sunlight Zone. This creature gets its name from its combs, which are the four rows of paddle-like hairs along its body that are used for swimming.

SEA WALNUTS

The sea walnut, known to scientists as the *Mnemiopsis leidyi*, is a bioluminescent comb jelly. It has an oval, see-through body and likes to live in shallow coastal waters. It is called a sea walnut because it is small, only 7 to 12 centimetres (3 to 5 inches) long, moves slowly, is blind, and has no brain. Despite that, it has survived so well that it is invading the habitats of other creatures. It doesn't have stinging cells, so it uses sticky mucus to catch its prey. It has **tentacles** that help it eat **zooplankton**, other comb jellies, fish eggs, and sometimes even other sea walnuts!

Even though it is blind and can't see light (even its own), it uses bioluminescence to protect itself. Its rows of combs running from top to bottom glow blue-green when it is disturbed. Being so small, one sea walnut does not make much light. But when gathered by the hundreds, the display is vast and bright.

The rainbow colours along the jelly's combs are caused by light hitting the moving hairs, not by its bioluminescence.

Most comb jellies, like this sea walnut, are see-through to help them stay invisible in the dim light of the Sunlight Zone.

16

CRYSTAL JELLIES

One of the predators a sea walnut might want to frighten away is the crystal jelly, which likes to snack on them. These jellies will also eat other crystal jellies if they are really hungry! It's a jelly-eat-jelly world in the sea. Crystal jellies have long, delicate tentacles around the edge of umbrella-shaped bodies. Along this edge, there are more than 100 tiny, light organs that flash green.

The crystal jelly has a distinctive way of making light. When the crystal jelly is disturbed, it first creates a blue light. Then, a green fluorescent protein (GFP) in its body turns that light green. Scientists have isolated the GFP gene and inserted it into other creatures, such as fish, mice, rabbits, insects, and even pigs, making them glow this same green. This protein acts like a highlighter to help scientists find and study genes.

The green ring of light that glows when the crystal jelly is disturbed only last a few seconds.

HOW TO MAKE GREEN MICE

Transferring genes from one organism to another is tricky business. Scientists take the dangerous **HIV** virus and strip it of the disease-carrying parts. This virus is special because it spreads by transferring its own genetic material into the host cell. The scientists then add the GFP protein to the HIV virus. They inject the now-harmless HIV virus into the single-cell **embryos** of mice. When the mice are born, they carry the florescent-green jellyfish gene in their own genetic material. Under fluorescent light, their entire bodies, and all their organs, give off a green glow.

The green glow in the two mice who have the GFP protein can only be seen under UV light and does not hurt them.

DON'T GO THERE

Why is it so difficult for scientists to study sea jellies?

1. Sea jellies are almost completely made of water, so there are few fossils available to use in order to learn their history.
2. When they are taken out of the ocean, they turn to blobs of goo that are hard to examine.
3. They are fragile. Many will explode when they are touched, so it is almost impossible to catch them in a net.
4. They often live deep in the ocean where there is too much pressure for humans to dive.
5. Some types are extremely poisonous to humans.
6. Jellyfish can still sting even when they are dead.

CHAPTER 4

The Twilight Zone

Farther down in the sea, in the Twilight Zone, light from the sun begins to fade. Marine animals here need to get creative with light in order to eat before they get eaten.

LARGEST MIGRATION ON EARTH

Many creatures living in this zone are part of what scientists call the Deep Scattering Layer. This layer is made up of large groups of organisms that **migrate** up and down in the sea each day. At night, when other predators are less alert and the darkness gives them some cover, they swim up to feed. When the sunlight brightens the water again during the day, they swim deeper to rest and hide. Over 10 billion tons of living matter make this trip each day, making it the largest migration on Earth.

SONAR SURPRISE

This vertical migration wasn't discovered until the 1940s when the US Navy was taking **sonar** readings of the ocean floor. The band of creatures is so thick in the Deep Scattering Layer that the sonar would bounce off them, making researchers think it was the bottom of the ocean. As they continued their readings, the navy noticed that the bottom of the ocean seemed to be shallower during the night and deeper during the day. Since the ocean floor clearly wasn't moving, they knew there had to be another explanation. By dropping **tow nets** and sending researchers down in **submersibles**, the Deep Scattering Layer was discovered.

IN LIVING COLOUR

The Japanese firefly squid is one of the creatures that makes the daily Deep Scattering Layer migration. It is about 7.6 centimetres (3 inches) long when fully grown and only lives for about one year. While it is alive, it is part of a great bioluminescent light show. This squid has light-producing cells called photophores

USE OF BIOLUMINESCENCE

Japanese firefly squid glow to lure prey to their tentacles and to attract mates.

The firefly squid has large photophores in the ends of its tentacles and around its eyes. It also has thousands of tiny photophores over the rest of its body.

all over its body. Large photophores are at the end of each of its eight tentacles and around its eyes. It also has thousands of tiny photophores all over its body so it can give off light from its entire form.

When the squid lays eggs from March to June each year, the waves in Toyama Bay, Japan, push them to the surface and send them towards land. The shoreline is bathed in a brilliant blue light from the thousands of small squid that flicker and flash in beautiful patterns of light.

Japanese firefly squid are the only squid that have colour vision. They have three **pigments** in parts of their **retina**, which scientists believe allow them to see different colours of light, although they only make blue light.

HIDE IN PLAIN SIGHT

Fish in the Sunlight Zone are constantly on the lookout for danger overhead. Many fish even have their eyes positioned on the top of their head for a better look in that direction. So if these fish want to sneak up on their dinner, how do they do it without creating a shadow that their prey swimming below them can see? The velvet belly lanternshark has figured out a way using bioluminescence.

RING TONE

While there are many types of bio-luminescent squid, there are few bioluminescent examples in their distant cousin, the octopus. One of the few is the *Japetella diaphana*, which is about 12 centimetres (4.7 inches) long and lives in warm ocean waters. Females have a bio-luminescent ring-shape around their mouths that give off a greenish light. Scientists believe they use it to attract males when they are ready to mate.

Scientists have just discovered that this shark also has photophores along the tip of its dorsal fin—like a light saber used to discourage predators.

Glow-in-the-Dark Firefly Squid Necklace

You can capture the beauty of bioluminescent light with your own glow-in-the-dark firefly squid pendant.

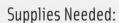

Supplies Needed:
- ✦ oven-bake clay (Fimo or Sculpey)
- ✦ wax paper
- ✦ tools for shaping (bamboo skewers or toothpicks)
- ✦ baking pan
- ✦ glow-in-the-dark paint
- ✦ eye pin

Instructions:

1. On wax paper, shape dough to form a squid body. Roll out more dough to make 8 arms and 2 tentacles. Attach to body.

2. Flatten a small white ball of clay for each eye. Use a smaller black ball or black bead for the centre of the eye.

3. Carefully insert the eye pin into the end of the squid if you want to make a pendant.

4. With the help of an adult, bake dough in the oven following the manufacturer's directions. Let cool.

5. Using the glow-in-the-dark paint, cover the squid's body with dots. Let dry.

6. Put your squid in the sunlight to absorb the light. Now go into a dark room or under black light and watch the light show!

SMART SHARKS

The velvet belly lanternshark is a member of the dogfish shark family. It is small at only about 45 centimetres (18 inches) long, and it has a stout body with a long nose and tail. Its body is brown all over except for the bottom of its belly. There, it has a black patch that is covered in light-producing cells called photophores.

This is the velvet belly lanternshark's ingenious camouflage. It uses a trick called counter-illumination. By turning on the lights as it swims, a fish swimming below it will look up and instead of seeing its predator's shadow, it will see blue light that blends into the sky. It will think the coast is clear, but the velvet belly lanternshark is there, hiding in plain sight.

FIRE-BREATHING SHRIMP

Shrimp are small arthropods, creatures who have their skeletons on the outside of their bodies in the form of shells or hard coverings. They can't dart away quickly like fish if they see a predator coming—they have to protect them-selves with different **tactics**.

While these shrimp are busy hunting down small **crustaceans** called krill to eat for lunch, octopuses, fish, sharks, and rays are looking to have them for a nice light snack. *Parapandalus* shrimp have developed a clever way of escaping danger using bioluminescence. When a predator attacks, the shrimp spews out bright, shining liquid as a distraction. Almost like a magician that disappears off the stage in a puff of smoke, this shrimp uses shock and surprise to make its escape.

USE OF BIOLUMINESCENCE

This shark uses bioluminescence as camouflage in order to hide its shadow with counter-illumination.

USE OF BIOLUMINESCENCE

Shrimp spit out glowing liquid as a distraction for a quick escape.

The bioluminescent fluid isn't blue when it is inside the shrimp—it only turns blue when the luciferin in the liquid reacts with the oxygen in the water.

ALARM JELLYFISH

Atolla jellyfish live in oceans around the world. They use their bioluminescence to survive. When an Atolla jellyfish is attacked, it sends out blue flashes to alert nearby predators that the fish, which is attacking it, would make a delicious dinner. The jellyfish's skills have earned it the nickname "alarm jellyfish."

BIOLUMINESCENT BAIT

Dr. Edith Widder is a marine biologist at the Ocean Research & Conservation Association. She has made hundreds of dives to explore the ocean and its creatures. On her dives, she noticed that remote-operated vehicles and submersibles were noisy and often scared away the creatures she wanted to study. She was fascinated by the amount of bioluminescent creatures that treated her to a light show when she was quiet and hidden. She decided to try mounting a camera to a platform that didn't move to observe sea life. She also developed the eJelly, an electronic jellyfish. The eJelly imitated the bioluminescent light patterns of the Atolla jellyfish as a **lure**. She, and a team of other scientists, used both devices 966 kilometres (600 miles) off the coast of Japan in July 2012. They were successful beyond their wildest dreams: with their stationary camera and bioluminescent lure, they caught the world's first pictures of the giant squid in its natural habitat.

The Atolla jellyfish flashes its brilliant blue lights in a spiralling pattern.

Now You See It, Now You Don't

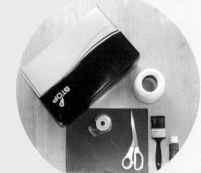

This activity will help you understand how bioluminescence helps fish hide in the sea. Predators that are looking up can see the silhouette of their prey because the fish block the sunlight with their bodies. By lighting up their bellies, the prey can mimic the missing sunlight and disguise their silhouettes.

Supplies Needed:
- ✦ shoebox
- ✦ string
- ✦ black construction paper
- ✦ needle
- ✦ tape
- ✦ black paint

Instructions:
1. Paint the inside of the shoebox black.

2. On one short side of the box, cut a small hole for viewing.

3. On the opposite short side of the box, prick several holes with the needle to let light in.

4. Cut two fish shapes out of black paper, small enough to fit inside the box. Prick one fish shape with the needle several times all over its body.

5. Attach a short piece of string to the top of each fish with tape and tape fish side by side to the underside of the lid so they hang down into the box.

6. Now look through the viewing hole. Which fish can you see more clearly?

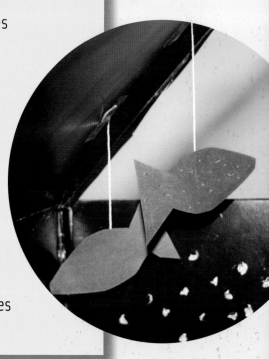

The fish with the holes in it allows the light behind it to shine through, making it difficult to see. The solid fish makes a black silhouette that gives away its location.

CHAPTER 5

USE OF BIOLUMINESCENCE

Anglerfish use bioluminescence as bait in order to catch prey.

The Deep

Sunlight cannot reach the deepest part of the ocean. Creatures that make the Midnight Zone (the Aphotic Zone) their home live in total and complete darkness. Scientists were astounded by how many creatures used bioluminescence here once they turned off their lights and had a look!

FATAL ATTRACTION

The anglerfish looks like a creature from a horror movie with its huge, gaping mouth full of needle-like teeth, short fat body, and dangling spike from its forehead. But good looks are not important in a world where no one can see you. What is important is to use what you have to survive in the Midnight Zone. The anglerfish has developed its bioluminescence in order to find its food.

The anglerfish goes fishing with its own built-in fishing pole. The spike on the anglerfish's forehead hangs down over its head near its mouth. It has a small bulb on the end that is full of bioluminescent bacteria that glow a blue-green light. The anglerfish stays motionless and waves the spike gently back and forth. Its prey is attracted to the light, and when it gets close, the anglerfish's huge jaws snatch it whole. In fact, the anglerfish's jaw can open so wide that it can swallow prey almost twice its own size!

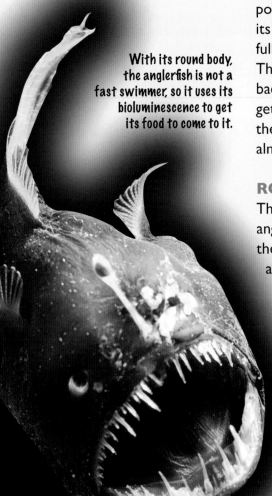

With its round body, the anglerfish is not a fast swimmer, so it uses its bioluminescence to get its food to come to it.

ROOM FOR RENT

The bioluminescent bacteria end up in the fleshy bulb of anglerfish through pores in the skin. Once inside the bulb, they settle in. Inside the bulb, they are protected, and they also get all their needed nutrients from their host. The bacteria and anglerfish have a symbiotic relationship, which means they both benefit from living together. The bacteria get free food and housing, and the anglerfish uses their bioluminescence to find prey.

MISSING MALES

Scientists noticed that only female anglerfish have these sharp teeth, huge jaws, and bioluminescent lures. For the longest time, they couldn't find male anglerfish at all. Then, they noticed that anglerfish seemed to have small fish attached to their sides. Researchers first thought they were some kind of parasite, but it turns out these tiny fish are actually the males! Male anglerfish spend their lives looking for a female and once they find one, they attach themselves to her **permanently**.

A VIEW TO A KILL

Another family of deep-sea fish that uses bioluminescent bacteria in its body is the flashlight fish.

These fish have two bean-shaped light organs just below their eyes. Inside are bioluminescent bacteria that perform the chemical reaction and glow a bright lime-green colour. The bacteria glow all the time, so different flashlight fish have developed different ways of turning off the light when they need to. One type of flashlight fish can rotate the photophores back into its body to mask the light. Other types have shutters that come down to cover the light and move back up when it's time to flash.

FLASH MOB

A school of flashlight fish can escape predators in a show of blinking confusion. When threatened, these fish flash their lights quickly, then zigzag away and flash again. With all of them doing this dance, the predator can't be sure where any one fish is. This system seems to work, because scientists have never found a flashlight fish in the stomach of a bigger fish.

These fish also flash to attract a tasty meal or send messages to other flashlight fish to either warn their neighbours of approaching predators or to find a mate. They usually flash two or three times a minute, but when they are in danger, they can blink up to 75 times a minute! At the very bottom of the deep sea, creatures have evolved their own ways of dealing with the darkness. By creating their own light, they are able to find food and escape predators in a world where the sunlight never shines, day or night.

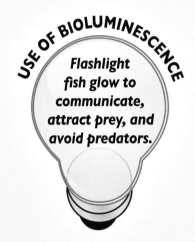

USE OF BIOLUMINESCENCE

Flashlight fish glow to communicate, attract prey, and avoid predators.

In parts of the Indian and Pacific Oceans, sailors follow the lights of flashlight fish in order to safely **navigate** through reef passes at night.

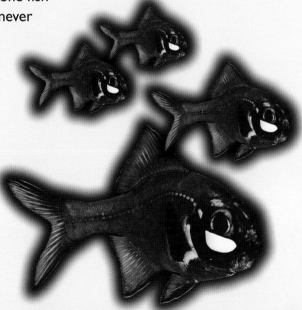

LIVING LARGE

The largest bioluminescent creature comes from the squid family. The *Taningia danae* is a deep-sea, eight-armed squid. The largest specimen ever found was a 161-kilogram (355-pound) female. This squid uses bioluminescent photophores on its arms to give off bright flashes of light to find and confuse its prey. It also uses flashing to frighten off its greatest threat—the sperm whale.

USE OF BIOLUMINESCENCE

The dragonfish's blue-green light attracts prey, while the red light allows it to see its prey without alerting it.

NIGHT VISION

One deep-sea fish has taken its bioluminescence to a whole new level. Most creatures in the ocean only produce blue-green light and only see blue-green light. But the deep-sea dragonfish has a special tool in its weaponry. It can create and see red light as well. As far as scientists know, the dragonfish is only one of very few creatures that have this ability.

The dragonfish is small at only 10 to 15 centimetres (4 to 6 inches) long. Along its body, and in a fleshy growth from its bottom jaw, called a barbell, are bioluminescent photophores that flash blue-green light.

It uses this blue-green light to attract prey, but the red light has a different purpose. Like a spy using night-vision glasses, the dragonfish uses its red light, created by special photophores under its eyes, to **illuminate** the sea around it to find food. The prey can't see the red light that is making them visible, and they swim merrily on their way—right into the dragonfish's mouth.

STUN GUN

Sea anemones look like flowers, but are actually animals. They are simple creatures that have a tube with a circle of small tentacles at one end and a foot to anchor themselves to the bottom of the ocean at the other end. The Venus flytrap sea anemone is named after the meat-eating plant of the same name because of the way it catches its food.

The dragonfish's stomach has black walls to keep the lights of its bioluminescent meal from shining through and making it a target for predators.

It has a funnel-shaped body and a large, disc-shaped mouth. Two rows of tentacles circle around the mouth, one row pointing outward and the other row sloping inward, like teeth. The Venus flytrap sea anemone turns its body so it faces the current and waits for food to drift by. Once the anemone senses a meal, the disc of mouth tentacles folds itself around its prey like a taco shell.

Because it can't swim, the anemone can't get away when a predator comes by. Instead, it uses its bioluminescence as a defense. When attacked, it spews out glowing mucus, hoping to distract its predator.

USE OF BIOLUMINESCENCE

The sea anemone secretes glowing mucus to defend against its predators.

The bioluminescent mucus from the Venus flytrap sea anemone sometimes sticks to an attacker, making it a glowing target.

RED LIGHT/ BLUE-GREEN LIGHT

Almost all bioluminescent light in the ocean is in the blue-green range, while much of the light produced on land is yellow or red. Why is that? It has to do with how light travels through air and water. In sea water, red light is **absorbed** quickly and does not travel far. Blue-green light travels the farthest, so it is the most useful for marine animals. On land, there isn't much difference in which light creatures can see, so red and yellow light is used by creatures such as fireflies and railroad worms.

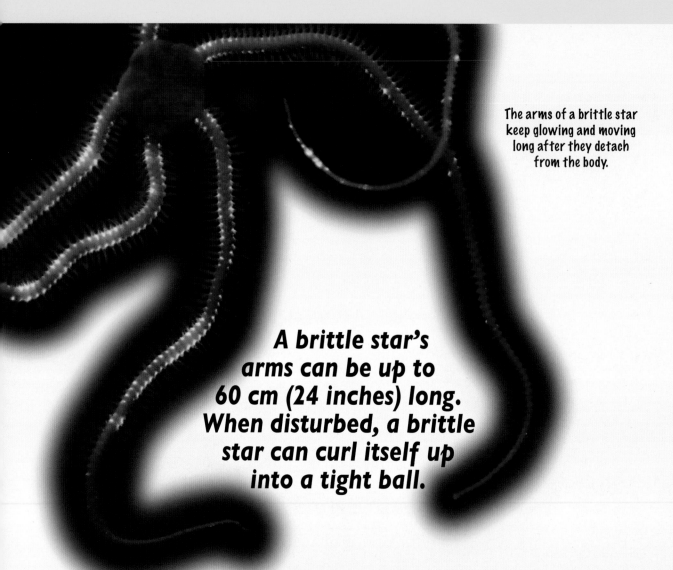

The arms of a brittle star keep glowing and moving long after they detach from the body.

A brittle star's arms can be up to 60 cm (24 inches) long. When disturbed, a brittle star can curl itself up into a tight ball.

USE OF BIOLUMINESCENCE

Brittle stars leave a glowing limb behind and make a quick escape.

LEND ME A HAND

Brittle stars are related to starfish, or sea stars, as they are sometimes called. Brittle stars usually have five arms, but where a starfish's arms are wide, the brittle star's arms are thin and whip-like. They use their arms to crawl along the seafloor by waving them around like moving snakes.

Crawling is not as fast as swimming, so brittle stars needed to develop a way to protect themselves from faster predators. Like most starfish and other brittle stars, they can re-grow their arms. Deep-sea brittle stars have added bioluminescence to this feature. Their arms have photophores, so when they are attacked, they leave behind a glowing arm called a sacrificial tag. The bioluminescent arm dazzles and distracts the attacker, while the brittle star has time to crawl away and grow a new one.

Light Scattering

See how particles in the water scatter different colours so a beam of light seems to change from yellow to blue.

Supplies Needed:
+ empty 2-litre pop bottle
+ flashlight
+ milk
+ water

Instructions:

1. Fill the 2-litre bottle 3/4 full of water and prop up the flashlight so it will shine through the bottle from the side in a darkened room.

2. Look at the beam of light. What colour is it?

3. Add a teaspoon of milk to the water, put the cap on and shake to mix the water and milk.

4. Now look at the beam of light again. What colour is the beam now?

5. Keep adding milk and check the colour of the beam. Is it changing?

CHAPTER 6

What's Next?

Bioluminescence is often called the "language of light" because it is a way to communicate without words. Creatures who can make and use their own cold light are able to send messages to other life forms to lure a meal, fight off predators, make a hasty escape, or find a mate.

Scientists who study bioluminescence are just beginning to unlock this evolutionary ability. While it is fairly rare on land, 80 to 90 percent of deep-sea creatures are able to make their own light. This shows researchers that it is a **vital** tool for survival for many animals. By understanding the chemical reaction and genes used to produce bioluminescence, researchers are finding new ways to harness this power.

MILITARY USES

The military is looking at ways to use this technology to make their work safer. One idea is to develop bioluminescent landing-zone markers for helicopters. Often, the whirling blades kick up a lot of dirt and debris and make it hard for pilots to land safely. Bioluminescent markers would shine through the debris and light up the field. This type of

Bioluminescent markers would make nighttime landings safer, especially during power outages.

light is also **biodegradable**, which means it won't pollute or leave anything toxic on the ground, like some paints.

The military might also use bioluminescence to mark team members. This could prevent accidental shootings during times of poor visibility. The military could use bioluminescent markers to identify important buildings or targets, too.

PROTECTING OUR WATER SUPPLY

Scientists are also using bioluminescent bacteria to test for toxins in water. They have developed microorganisms that glow when a chemical is present. The bacteria could be **modified** so that their light gets brighter when the poison, arsenic, or pollution, such as oil, is present in the water.

Another use scientists are investigating is the development of crops that turn on their bioluminescence to signal when they are drying out. This would mean that farmers would water their crops only when necessary, which could mean bigger crops and less wasted water.

WHO'S DOWN THERE?

Marine biologists are also using bioluminescence for a deep-sea population count. Most of the time, sea life is discovered and counted by dragging huge nets across the ocean floor and bringing creatures to the surface. Many animals that have adapted to living in extreme pressure, cold, and dark, die and **disintegrate** during this process. Scientists have developed a database of bioluminescent flash patterns that allow them to identify different species of animals. By lowering a silent, still camera, they can do a more accurate count of the diversity of life on the bottom of the ocean without harming any creatures.

POWERING OUR WORLD

Researchers are looking for ways to use bioluminescence to replace our dependence on electricity. One idea is to engineer glowing trees to replace streetlights. These trees would absorb sunlight during the day to provide the energy to glow all night. They would only need air, water, and soil to provide their light. Scientists say that the difficulty will be creating bioluminescent trees that glow bright enough to be useful as streetlights.

Scientists are investigating the possibility of using bioluminescence to develop plants that signal when they are fighting disease or under attack from pests.

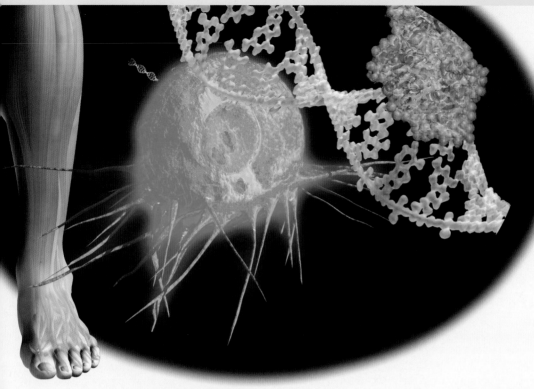

In 2008, the Nobel Prize for chemistry was awarded to three scientists, Shimomura, Chalfie, and Tsien, who first discovered GFP and its usefulness in marking genes for medical research.

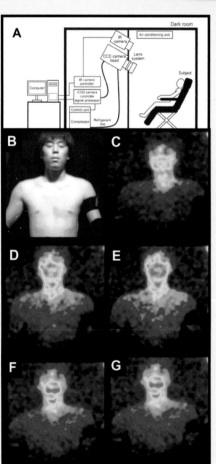

THE FIGHT AGAINST DISEASE

Scientists are using the enzyme luciferase to help them in the fight against muscular dystrophy. This disease causes muscles all over the body to weaken. Researchers add the luciferase gene to stem cells inside the muscles of mice with the disease. Then they look for the green glow that shows where the cells are actively repairing damaged muscles. By following the amount and change in the glowing areas, researchers can see if new drugs and therapies are slowing the destruction of muscle tissue, which will help people suffering from the disease.

GLOWING HUMANS

Japanese scientists have used an ultra-sensitive camera to capture the first images of human bioluminescence. The light we produce is faint—a thousand times weaker than our eyes can see. Scientists believe our faint glow is the result of chemical reactions in our body. The amount of energy we produce changes throughout the day following our **circadian rhythm**, which explains why we glitter brightest in the afternoon, and faintest at night.

Glossary

ABSORB soak up

ALGAL BLOOM thousands of tiny organisms called algae, which suddenly multiply

BECKONING using a gesture to encourage someone to come near or follow

BIODEGRADABLE material that will break down over time without harming the earth

CIRCADIAN RHYTHM a daily cycle of rising and falling activity in all living organisms

CRUSTACEANS sea creatures that have hard outer shells and limbs with joints, such as crabs, lobsters, and shrimp

DISINTEGRATE to break up into parts

DISTRACT turn someone's attention away from something

EMBRYOS unborn offspring

EVOLVE develop gradually over time

FORAGER an animal that searches for food

HIV the virus that causes AIDS, which is a disease that destroys a person's immune system leaving them open to dangerous infections and tumors

ILLUMINATE light up

INGENIOUS clever and inventive

LURE to tempt something

MIGRATE to move from one region to another

MODIFY make small changes

MOLECULE a group of atoms bonded together

MORSE CODE a code in which letters are represented by combinations of long and short sound signals

NAVIGATE to plan and direct the route of a ship

NOCTURNAL active at night

PENETRATE to pass into or through

PERMANENTLY lasting forever

PIGMENTS the natural colours in plant or animal cells

PREDATOR an animal that preys on other animals

QUORUM a group

RETINA the cells at the back of the eye that are sensitive to light

SONAR a system that uses sound pulses to measure the depth of water

SPECTACLE a grand display or performance

SUBMERSIBLE a small vehicle designed to work underwater

SURVEYOR a person who examines and measures positions on the earth's surface

TACTIC a carefully planned action

TENTACLE a bendable limb on squid used for grasping and moving

TOW NETS nets that are dragged along slowly behind a boat

TOXIC poisonous

VITAL absolutely necessary

ZOOPLANKTON small creatures that drift along in seas, oceans, and fresh water

Index

Further Reading

Books:

Barkan, Joanne. *Creatures That Glow*. New York: Doubleday Books for Young Readers, 1991.

Collard III, Sneed B. *A Firefly Biologist at Work*. New York: Scholastic Library Publishing, 2001.

Dunn, Mary R. *Fireflies*. North Mankato, MN: Capstone Press, 2012.

Lunis, Natalie. *Glow-in-the-dark Animals*. New York: Bearport Publishing, 2011.

Sitarski, Anita. *Cold Light: Creatures, Discoveries, and Inventions That Glow*. Honesdale, PA: Boyds Mill Press, 2007.

Websites:

"All About the Firefly." http://www.firefly.org/facts-about-fireflies.html

"San Diego Natural History Museum's 'Lights Alive'." http://www.sdnhm.org/archive/kids/lightsalive/index.html

"Scientific American's Gallery of Bioluminescent Creatures." http://www.scientificamerican.com/slideshow.cfm?id=bioluminescent-avatar

"Take a bioluminescent exploration dive with Dr. Edith Widder." http://www.teamorca.org/cfiles/biolum_landing.cfm

"VIDEO: *National Geographic*: Bioluminescence on Camera." http://www.youtube.com/watch?v=9HXXQBz6Vv0

Bibliography

Books:

Shimomura, Osamu. *Bioluminescence: Chemical Principles and Methods*. Singapore: World Scientific Publishing, 2012.

Wilson, Therese and J. Woodland Hastings. *Bioluminescence: Living Lights, Lights for Living*. Cambridge, MA: Harvard University Press, 2013.

Videos:

"Dr. Paul Marek on bioluminescent millipedes." http://www.youtube.com/watch?v=ivU0YdlE7E4

"Edith Widder: How we found the giant squid: TED Talk." http://www.ted.com/talks/edith_widder_how_we_found_the_giant_squid.html

Websites:

"The Bioluminescence Web Page." http://www.lifesci.ucsb.edu/~biolum/

"National Oceanic and Atmospheric Administration, Bioluminescence."
   http://oceanexplorer.noaa.gov/explorations/09bioluminescence/background/bioluminescence/bioluminescence.html

"Ocean Research & Conservation Association." http://www.teamorca.org

Exhibits:

"Creatures of Light Exhibit." The Field Museum, Chicago, 2013.

Image Credits